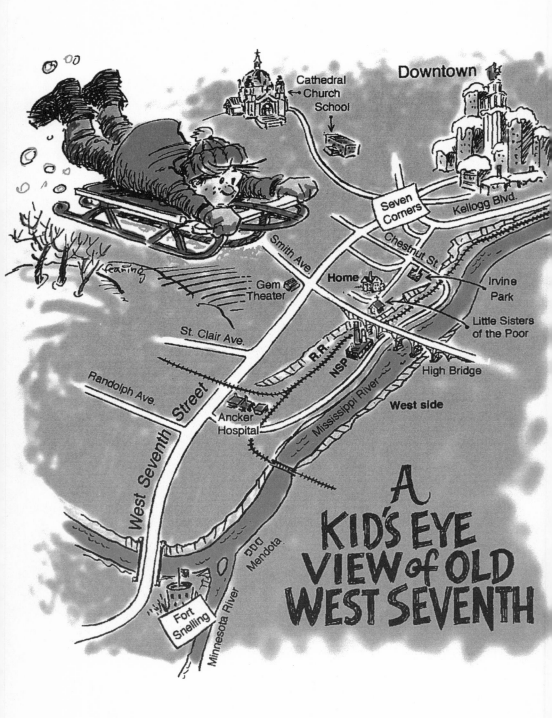

CHRISTMAS on WEST SEVENTH STREET

CHRISTMAS on WEST SEVENTH STREET

By Jerry Fearing

Afton Historical Society Press
Afton, Minnesota

Designed by Mary Susan Oleson
Edited by Sarah P. Rubinstein

Library of Congress Cataloging-in-Publication Data

Fearing, Jerry.
    Christmas on West Seventh Street / by Jerry Fearing. -- 1st ed.
        p. cm.
    ISBN 1-8900434-31-0
    I. Fearing, Jerry--Childhood and youth. 2. Saint Paul (Minn.)--
Social life and customs--20th century. 3. Saint Paul (Minn.)--Biography.
4. Christmas--Minnesota--Saint Paul. I. Title.

F614.S4 F28 2000
977.6'581053--dc21

                                                                00-056582

Printed in Canada

The Afton Historical Society Press publishes
exceptional books on regional subjects.

W. Duncan MacMillan   Patricia Condon Johnston
        president   publisher

Afton Historical Society Press
P.O. Box 100
Afton, MN 55001
800-436-8443
aftonpress@aftonpress.com
www.aftonpress.com

To Dick, Chuck, Nick, Bobby, and Peter,
the guys I ran with on
Old West Seventh

This is the fifth annual
holiday book
published by the
Afton Historical Society Press

Earlier titles include:

AN ADOLESCENT'S CHRISTMAS
by Carol Bly

UNDERGROUND CHRISTMAS
by Jon Hassler

FACES OF CHRISTMAS PAST
by Bill Holm

*CHRISTMAS AND NEW YEAR'S
ON THE MINNESOTA FRONTIER*
by Bertha Heilbron

CHRISTMAS on WEST SEVENTH STREET

CHRISTMAS MEMORIES are personal and therefore different for each of us. Every generation has its own setting, a time and place that can never be again. While the act of physically growing up doesn't change much, the world around us does. These indelible memories of home, school friends, and activities in childhood are stamped on us for life. Whether it was on a farm or in the city or a small town, growing up was a scary, mysterious, sometimes heart-breaking, often joyful experience.

Still I'm sure that certain aspects of this special Christmas are universal enough that even those who were not around in 1940, the setting for these reminiscences, will be able to identify with our story.

This was the year of the infamous Armistice Day Blizzard in which many lives were lost and everyone was snowed under for days. But as far as I was concerned, it was just another big storm that started the winter off with plenty of snow.

The year 1940 was also the year Franklin D. Roosevelt ran for his third term against Wendell Willkie. That was the first election I was to take an interest in. Roosevelt was given credit in our house for leading us out of the Depression. So, of course, we voted Democratic. I even drew cartoons for the occasion. One of them got me into trouble with the nuns when I put it up on the bulletin board at school. It was really more of an illustration than a political cartoon. I illustrated a popular slogan from the election campaign: "A Horse's Tail is Silky, Lift It Up And You'll Find Willkie!"

THE WORLD was at war at the time, and we were surrounded with propaganda calling on the United States to join in the fight. The Germans, Italians, and Japanese were the bad guys. They had to be destroyed. The country entered the war after Pearl Harbor was bombed on December 7, 1941.

My dad was too old for the draft (he ended up welding ship parts for the navy), and I had no older brothers or sisters in the service. So for me, at age ten, it was an impersonal, distant war, happening to other people somewhere else in the world. Despite all I heard about battles won or lost in the newsreels, it didn't seem to involve me. I certainly didn't pay much attention to the newspaper accounts; my only interest was in reading the comics. Later on I collected scrap metal, and we saved lard for the war effort and soon learned to live with rationing. But despite all that was going on elsewhere, the center of my world remained the family and the neighborhood.

I grew up in an area known as West Seventh in St. Paul, Minnesota. Seventh Street ran through downtown St. Paul, southwest all the way to old Fort Snelling, which was a military post built beginning in 1819 at the confluence of the Minnesota and Mississippi Rivers. Neighborhoods along Seventh Street west of downtown were made up of a mixture of lower to lower-middle-class Irish, Swedish, Bohemian, German, Italian, and Jewish families. For me and my younger sister and brother, home was the rented upstairs of a duplex on Wilkin Street.

I didn't roam far from home in those days. We had everything we needed close by. Church, playgrounds, grocery store, drugstore, bakery, even the neighborhood movie theater were all within walking distance of home. Of course, walking distance then covered a lot more area than it does today. Now we drive to the store or church and are bussed to school. In those days we walked!

A kid soon learned if he wandered out of his own area into some of the tougher neighborhoods he could find himself in trouble!

I walked to school each day. It was the Cathedral Elementary School located a couple of miles from home on Kellogg Boulevard (tuition was fifty cents a month). There seemed to be an unwritten truce that allowed kids to pass through other neighborhoods to and from school without a problem. However, after school, on weekends, or during vacation when we ventured onto another's turf, it often meant a fight or a hasty retreat.

In our circle, kids and adults lived very separate lives. For recreation after work my dad went bowling, played cards at the corner saloon, or went with my mom to visit friends. None of these activities included kids. There were few nearby family restaurants and no fast food places, so we never went out as a family to eat.

No matter what was going on, we always stopped to gather at home for supper.

We were also expected to be back in the house at dark. If I was slow at bringing an end to the game, Mom was at the back door calling to remind me, "It's getting late!"

By the time I was ten, my activities went pretty much unsupervised. Younger kids were reluctantly looked after by older brothers and sisters.

Adults had their secrets and so did we! We could tell by the way conversation slowed up or even stopped when a kid walked into a room of adults that they had been discussing something we weren't supposed to know about. So we kept our daily adventures a secret from them. It was probably better for their peace of mind that they didn't know what we were up to. There's the time I lost my grip on a rope while swinging out over the hillside above Pleasant Avenue near St. Clair Street. I came crashing down through the trees to hit

the ground in a tangle of broken branches. Miraculously nothing on me was broken, but Mom couldn't understand how most of my body and face could get covered with scratches and bruises from just running around in the woods.

Sometimes we skated or went to the playgrounds. Most often football was played on any grassy open spot we could find but our softball field was the street. Traffic was so light we seldom had to stop the game more than two or three times to let a car pass. For hockey we cleared the snow off a pond we called Kahoots that was located under the High Bridge.

Since we had no guards or pads of any kind, we had to play with care. Still the sticks and puck left our lower legs black and blue.

If the Saturday afternoon movie was a Tarzan flick, we played "jungle" for the next week. If it was a western, then we became cowboys.

GETTING READY FOR THE HOLIDAY

THEN, AS NOW, the religious significance of Christ's birthday was the last thing on a kid's mind. It was the colorful trappings, the Santa legend, and *GIFTS* that captured and held our attention. Preparations for the big day started soon after Thanksgiving. Wreaths went up on doors, electric candles appeared in the windows, and soon through those windows could be seen Christmas trees glittering in living rooms. In my memory, the scene seems to glow like a Terry Redlin painting.

Maybe it's because I stood closer to the ground then, but the snow in our yard and on the streets seemed a lot deeper in those days. There wasn't much snow removal at that time so the snow cleared from streets, sidewalks, and driveways ended up as huge mounds along the curbs. Playing on these was as close as we kids ever got to mountain climbing.

There were none of the glitzy-blinking lights in yards or along roofs that we see today. Nor did I see Santa's sleigh on rooftops or hear loud speakers blaring Christmas music at the neighbors'. It was more subdued, less commercial. For me a sure sign that Christmas wasn't far off was being asked to draw pictures on the school blackboards. The teacher knew I spent most of my time drawing pictures anyway, so she put me to work going from room to room drawing Christmas scenes in colored

chalk. Because I attended a parochial school, I usually chose as my subject the three wise men on their camels, Bethlehem with a big star shining above it, or the manger scene with animals. I enjoyed the assignment because it kept me out of class where

I was supposed to be learning something about long division and spelling.

Then there were the lists of things we wanted for Christmas or what we hoped to buy as gifts for members of the family.

We didn't have the newspaper supplements from shopping centers with stores like Toys "R" Us. But we did have catalogs from Wards and Sears. My four-year-old brother, six-year-old sister, and I would spend hours on the front-room floor paging through them, oh-ing and ah-ing over the array of products pictured there.

Unfortunately we were Depression babies who grew up being told "we can't afford that!" So we knew most of the items pictured in the catalog were out of reach. Our lists were made up of inexpensive items, like books, fingernail polish, slippers, hair combs and brushes, and bubble bath or simple items of clothing like ties or handkerchiefs.

Mom helped the younger kids buy the items they wanted to give each other, but when you got to be as old as I, you were expected to save up your nickels and dimes and buy them yourself. Those nickels and dimes were hard to come by. There was no such a thing as an allowance at our house. You did your chores without pay. Nor did babysitting pay anything. I was expected to take and watch my little sister and brother when I went to the playground or to pull them along on the sled when I went sliding at Irvine Park. Running a special errand could earn you something. Shoveling snow for elderly neighbors was a good source of income during the winter months. You could earn a quarter if you did a good job, or even fifty cents if it was a corner lot. Another lucrative source of revenue was the front-room furniture. On the morning after our folks had entertained

friends at the house, we'd rush to the living-room couch and chair, remove the cushions, and search the furniture's lining for change that had slipped from the guests' pockets. It often paid very well.

I mentioned sliding at Irvine Park. That was one of our two favorite winter activities. The other was ice skating, which we did for the most part at Ramsey Playground.

To us kids it was known as "Erving Park." It held the remnants of a stylish old area that once even had a fountain in the center. A high hill swept down from the

west through the trees. Huge houses that were once home to the elite of St. Paul circled the park. But at the time we used the hill for sliding, the area had become just a deteriorating lower-middle-class neighborhood. Years later it was discovered by a new generation. The old houses were renovated, and today Irvine Park again reflects some of the glory of those early years. We kids knew nothing of the park's past. For us it was just one of the few good hills in the area for sliding.

We used runner sleds and toboggans but the best ride was had with a large piece of cardboard curled back over the knees of the kids in front. As it started down the hill kids would come running and jump on. By the time it came to a stop at the bottom, the giggling mass was at least three-kids high.

I must tell you of the greatest sled ride in the history of "Erving Park." One night a

freezing rain had left everything coated with
a half inch of ice! A handful of us kids
showed up at the park the next morning
before the city got around to treating the

streets. From the top of the hill, we belly flopped down through the park, over the curb, and down the block to Chestnut Street. There we made a sharp right turn and sped down Chestnut Hill, across the railroad tracks, all the way down to the Mississippi River. It must have been at least an eight-block run. I think of that ride every time I see the bobsleds in the Olympics on TV. We hurriedly made the long slippery walk back to the park for another go at it. By the time we got back the trucks had arrived, spreading cinders in the street and putting an end to our glorious sled ride.

As I said, I usually had to bring my sister and brother along sliding. I hated that. It was pretty cold on that windy hill, but when you're busy climbing back up and running around, it didn't bother you much. My sister was old enough to handle it. But my little brother, who was too young and

34

over-dressed to be very active, was a problem. I would slide and fool around with my friends, ignoring his complaints as best I could. Finally his crying would start drawing attention. So I'd put him back on the sled and pull him home. By the time I got him there and upstairs, his feet and hands were painfully cold. While Mom held his feet and massaged warmth back into him, she'd scold me for not taking better care of him. My answer, of course, was not to send him along in the first place. As I look back now, I realize what a painfully miserable experience it must have been to be my little brother.

SHOPPING

BECAUSE I WAS THE OLDEST, I was picked to go along with my mother to help with the Christmas shopping. My dad took no part in such things. We left right after supper, walking the couple miles from Wilkin Street down Exchange Street to Kellogg Boulevard and into downtown St. Paul. We could have gone up to Seventh Street and taken a streetcar to town, but that would have taken precious dimes that were better spent on presents.

The nights were still and seemed awful

cold as we crunched along. But the excitement and fast pace kept it from bothering us.

The stores would be warm. Before we went into them, however, we had to walk around viewing the store windows. Schuneman's, the Emporium, and the Golden Rule all filled their windows with moving dioramas that brought to life the story of Dickens's Christmas Carol or Disney's Snow White. I also remember Santa's workshop with the elves busily painting and packing up gifts while Santa sat there nodding his head as he checked his list.

We went into all the stores, including Field-Schlick and Husch Brothers. When it came to my gift list, I did my buying in stores like Bannon's, Grant's, Woolworth's, and the other dime stores that lined Seventh Street. I was most impressed in these stores by the candy and toy counters. The toy counter must have run twenty feet or more down the aisle, filled with toys on both sides. There were tin and cast iron planes, trucks, and cars, wooden paddles with small rubber balls attached with long binders, spy glasses, pocket knives, colorful tops, and all kinds of wind-up toys, this being long before the day of the battery-operated toy. It was also before plastic, so the brightly painted little soldiers, cowboys and Indians were usually made of lead.

The glass-fronted candy counter contained bin after bin of candies in bulk. There were colorful hard Christmas candies with soft centers, multi-color striped ribbon candy, chocolate creams, chocolate Santas, and on and on it went. Only the expensive chocolates were boxed. The rest of it came in bulk so you could buy as little or as much as you could afford. Within a year or so most of this would disappear when the war made sugar and chocolate scarce.

If all went well, before starting the long hike home we stopped at the dime-store lunch counter for a ten-cent malt. As I remember, it came in a tall glass, a thick chocolate-flavored whipped milk. It was probably the forerunner of today's Dairy Queen.

Then we'd start for home, arms filled with packages. When the cold got to our toes and fingers, we stopped, put the packages down, and jumped around, clapping our hands together till we warmed up. As we walked, we talked of many things. We talked about school and why my last report card had been so bad. Mom liked the pictures I drew but thought it would be better if I spent as much time doing homework on important subjects as I did drawing. Of course, I told her I would. But I was most interested in talking about what I wanted for Christmas. And what I wanted more than anything else in the world was a

chemistry set! They were made by Gilbert and contained all kinds of exotic chemicals in little wooden containers along with test tubes, a pipette, and a small stand to hold it all. Mom didn't think much of the idea. According to her I'd probably blow up the house or at least burn it down. Then came the final blow. They were expensive, and we couldn't afford it now, maybe next year. There was no effective rebuttal to that argument.

THE TREE

MY FATHER'S ONE contribution to the holiday season, aside from paying the bills, was taking us out to buy the tree. We all went along, kind of like today when the whole family drives out into the country to pick out and cut its own tree. We didn't have far to go. Just a few blocks from the house, a fellow had brought in a truckload of trees and turned his front yard into a tree lot. I don't remember any flocked trees then and very few long-needled ones. Most were of the short-needle variety and

sold for a buck or two. The trick was to find a nice rounded tree that might hold most of its needles until after the holiday.

Some waited to put up their trees till Christmas Eve. We usually put ours up in the living room the same day we brought it home and left it up for a couple of weeks. As soon as we got it inside, it went into a three-legged stand with the bottom of the tree in a pot of water, which was filled every day for as long as the tree stayed inside. There was always the concern of fire with a dry tree as well as the needles falling off prematurely. The big box of decorations came down from the attic, and we all pitched in. First Dad tested the string of large lights with reflectors. If one bulb was burned out, none of them would light! Next came the colored paper chains we kids had made in school. Then we carefully hung the delicate glass ornaments on the branches. Finally it was all draped in glittering tinsel. The lights were then plugged in, the room lights were turned off, and we stood in awe of the beauty we'd created. When the room lights were turned on again, I noticed the needles were already falling.

THE PHANTOM
GIFT OPENER

A S SOON AS WE BROUGHT HOME the things we planned to give as presents, they were wrapped up in new Christmas wrapping paper and hidden away in a closet. There they stayed until the big night when they joined Santa's gifts under the tree. It was a pretty good system. Our parents thought that with the presents out of sight we kids wouldn't spend our time worrying about them.

But this particular year, someone went into the closet and tore open all the packages just enough to see what they contained! Satisfied, the Phantom stacked up the presents, torn paper and all, and disappeared. When my mother discovered the skullduggery, she questioned each of us. No one would admit having done it. Mother repaired the wrappings, stacked them on a higher shelf in the closet, and said no more about it. To this day the Phantom goes unpunished. My sister and I were outraged by the injustice of it all. We talked it over and agreed we hadn't done it. So we had a pretty good idea who the culprit was who got away with this heinous crime.

THE BIG DAY

AT THAT TIME CHRISTMAS was the most exciting day of the year in a kid's life. The Fourth of July ran a close second because fireworks were then legal. We could bicycle across the High Bridge to the West Side and buy them at the road-side stands. But Christmas was a special event for the whole family. And it lasted longer. There were days of anticipation and preparation. Then the excitement lingered long afterward while the polish wore off our new treasures.

That year we spent Christmas at my Mother's brother's house. (We had a great day with Uncle Joe and his family.) There was a cousin about my age in the family so we played board games and even went out to run around in the snow. I'm sure a wonderful meal was served, but I don't remember much about it. What held my attention that day was the candy! Uncle Joe worked at a candy factory. It seemed that everywhere in the house there were bowls of rich, delicious chocolates. Every time my sister or I passed one, we helped ourselves to a sample. By day's end, she was sick, and I too was turning green and felt I might give up candy for the rest of my life.

❄   ❄   ❄

FOR US KIDS, the big day had started early. Just before dawn, we'd rushed into

the living room. There under the tree were the much-anticipated presents. It didn't take long to get them all opened. The floor was soon littered with ribbons and wrapping paper. There were wool socks, robes, and slippers. But it was the toys and games that caught our eye. I remember a metal cowboy on a horse that whirled a wire lasso over his head and a wind-up train that sped around a tin landscape. I recall the train especially because the first

thing I did was cut my finger on a sharp edge of it. My sister, of course, received the mandatory doll. There was also a porcelain tea set, jigsaw puzzles, and books about Black Beauty and Treasure Island. My brother received a cowboy outfit with belt, holsters, and a couple of shiny cap pistols.

The gift that year that will always live in my memory was there under the tree with my name on it. It was a big wooden box labeled CHEMISTRY SET. It was all there—the test tubes and exotic chemicals. It even had a book describing experiments that wouldn't blow up the house or even burn it down. But it did tell me how to create a most wonderfully foul odor, powerful enough to stink up the entire neighborhood.

❉   ❉   ❉

In making these drawings and jotting down my memories, I realize just how much of this special year of my childhood I've lost. Only these few highlights are still with me. Most of the details have faded away into mental oblivion. But then, each year I have the opportunity to replace those lost memories with new ones. After all, Christmas comes around every year.

About the Author

JERRY FEARING has been drawing pictures for as long as he can remember. For more than forty years he was staff artist and cartoonist for the *St. Paul Pioneer Press and Dispatch*. His books include *The Sioux Uprising*, *The Story of Minnesota*, *That Wild Campaign of '68*, and *Fearing Revisited—Twenty Years of Cartoons*.

Except for a stint with the Marine Corps during the Korean War, Fearing has always lived in or close to St. Paul. "This acorn never rolled far from the tree and my roots in West Seventh have always drawn me back to the old neighborhood," he says. Now retired from the newspaper, he and his wife Dolores live in Scandia, a small community north of St. Paul.

Designed by
Mary Susan Oleson
Nashville, Tennessee

Typeface is
Trump Mediaeval